Reflexology: The   ok

By Kaı

Disclaimer: This book is not intended as a substitute for the medical advice of physicians. The reader should regularly consult a physician in matters relating to his/her health, and particularly with respect to any symptoms that may require medical diagnosis or medical attention.

Cover by Kane Georgiou.

Table of Contents

Chapter 1

Introduction - What will I learn from this book?

The distinguishing quality of this book is that it sums together many different perspectives on reflexology, while at the same time priding a coherent, structured and straightforward account that can readily prepare you to either give reflexology a try or just answer some basic questions about this complimentary alternative practice. You may be wondering why does some research **prove reflexology** while other studies deny it, what does a **regular session** look like or **who can it help**? If these are the kind of questions on your mind, brew yourself some tea or coffee, find a comfortable spot and jump straight to the chapter title that really caught your attention. Take a peak and then judge for yourself.

Starting with *Chapter 2*, you'll become acquainted with the complexity of reflexology, what sets it apart from a simple foot massage, as well as concrete proof of its impact upon our mood and lifestyle. You don't need to be sick to enjoy its benefits, but if you do suffer from a specific condition, you might find it in the list of disorders for which the impact of this CAM was thoroughly researched and proven. The "juicy" part of this chapter is the latter half, which talks about a dimension of healing that's been almost obliterated by modern medicine. So much so that an entire field was created to patch things up and take care of this basic need that patients have.

Chapter 3 talks about both the general and the specific health benefits of reflexology. Using a down-to-earth approach to the claims that are frequently associated with the practice, this section gives you the information you need to ascertain whether these claims have any grounds or whether they are an exaggeration. For example: Do you want to lose 10 pounds in 2 weeks? See a reflexologist. Do you want to heal your bunions or sinusitis? See a reflexologist. Some of these allegations may be true... to an extent. Starting from the medically proven, physiological effects that reflexology has on your lymphatic, circulatory and nervous systems, as well as the consequences that these changes have upon our psychology and brain chemistry, you'll be able to separate fact from fiction and *more accurately* determine whether it's possible to lose weight, heal your illness or anything else you might have heard from someone you know or from a TV show that's not particularly scrupulous with the allegations that it makes.

We've all heard myths and legends at one point or another. Does the freshwater lake in Scotland harbour a terrible monster that also goes by the friendly name Nessie? These are the obvious ones, but what do we do with the myths that arise out of lack of knowledge, misinformation or experiences with unqualified professionals? We must seek to find what brought them about in the first place and amend these mistakes with factual information and consistent arguments (not loud, but sound). This is where *Chapter 4* comes into discussion. It seeks to clarify some of the most common prejudices people have about reflexology by talking through what does and can happen during a session and what doesn't. Preview: No needles are used. Ever. Here, you might also find out some interesting facts about pharmaceuticals and illness.

Furthermore, if you really wish to understand reflexology, it's also important to know how it came to be as a theory and as a medical practice. Is it really true that people were practicing it thousands of years ago in Egypt and China? *Chapter 5* sheds some light on these matters, while also talking about the people who refined and improved reflexology into the powerful healing tool it is today. This section examines the scientific context that gave birth to Zone Therapy, the precursor to modern reflexology, as well as the core tenants that survive to this day.

If you still have some hesitations towards reflexology, *Chapter 6* will definitely improve your opinion of it and we owe it all to neurology. With the help of data from this field of activity, this chapter makes an incursion into the finer interactions that take place in our body during a session. At this point, you're slowly going to realize that balance, harmony and equilibrium are not just fancy words associated with Eastern beliefs, but actual physical processes that we rely on to survive. Towards the end, you'll also find out about the various reactions people can have as a result of a treatment and what causes them.

But we wanted this book to be more than an informative incursion into the field of reflexology. While the space constraints kept us from taking a much closer look at the anatomy underneath, *Chapter 7* nonetheless presents a reflexology diagram reference of your palms and feet. These colourful pictures express the associations that exist between certain points on our hands and feet and various organ systems within our body. While it may seem difficult to grasp at first, the physiology is accurate. In fact, this is what a qualified practitioner sees when they look at a patient. Still in *Chapter 7*, you'll also find some interesting facts about our feet and hands. This segment of the book really becomes useful when you use it in conjunction with the next chapter, which is a practical guide teaching you how to use a few basic reflexology techniques to relieve pain and stress without the help of conventional medication.

Therefore, *Chapter 8* breaks down a few routines in very easy, clear movements that can be performed by anyone either on themselves, a relative or a close acquaintance. Some of them are designed to help with migraines and back pains while others will help you deal with anxiety and tension better. This is where all of your knowledge will come to fruition, as these sequences will allow you to experience some of the benefits of reflexology without even scheduling a session. Always remember, however, that the effects and benefits are even more rewarding when you're under the care of a qualified professional. You may feel the urge to skip all the way to this chapter, but without all of the information leading up to it, you might end up working in the dark. Previous chapters will help you accurately determine what your movements are supposed to *trigger* or, for that matter, if what you're doing is helpful in any way.

Chapter 9 further develops reflexology techniques for individuals who are interested in spending more time harmonizing their body, preventing disease or ameliorating existing health problems. It is common for therapists to recommend that patients practice some of these routines at home, as a way to help themselves between sessions or in moments when their condition is overwhelming. This is the place where you need to look if you want to use reflexology in order to cope with heartburns, acne, asthma, Parkinson's or even osteoporosis. What you need to remember throughout this chapter and, indeed, through the entire book is that reflexology does not offer an instant fix to any health problem, but rather it works in conjunction with a holistic approach on health to assist your system in healing or fighting off the illness naturally, through its own mechanisms. Unlike *Chapter 8*, these techniques are more complex and involve routines that touch on multiple reflex points throughout the body. As such, a more significant time commitment is advisable if you desire them to be effective.

Last, but not least, we've decided to end our short incursion into reflexology with a chapter on complimentary healing, or things you can do to further aid your system to restore its balance. Reflexology itself is part of a holistic philosophy of healing, which supports that curing oneself is a multi-faceted process that requires changes on all levels, not only the strictly physical aspect. Consequently, reflexology works best when it is performed in conjunction with other useful practices. To this end, *Chapter 10* talks about the changes you can make to your diet, your lifestyle (particularly the way you deal with stress and anxiety), as well as to the amount of exercise you usually undergo in order to unlock the full potential of this complimentary alternative medicine.

Especially if you're someone who hasn't had much contact with this sort of medicine or holistic mentality, this book will definitely come in handy. Its goal is not to convince you to try reflexology, but rather to show you the evidence that delivers it from the undeserving stigma most of us regard it with. In addition, the practical additions to our description of reflexology allow you to try it out on your own before deciding to see an experienced practitioner or just out of sheer curiosity. Above anything else, each and every chapter was written with *love* and *care* for the reader – **you**. Whether you read 1 chapter or 10, our goal was to help you and we sincerely hope to achieve it.

Chapter 2

What is reflexology and how can it benefit me?

From a patient's perspective, reflexology is the application of pressure to specific points on your feet, ears or hands. This is not a working definition of reflexology as a practice, but one that we can relate to as readers who are unacquainted with the intricacies of this alternative therapy. On the whole, reflexology requires lengthy, specialized training, a very intricate understanding of human physiology in general and of the cardiovascular, lymphatic and nervous systems in particular, as well as specific knowledge of massaging techniques.

While you may look at your palm, ear lobe or foot as nothing more than a surface, a professional reflexologist sees a map of pressure points or reflex points that are connected to various organ systems in your body. When you touch your lover's hand or give them a foot massage, you may feel heat and, especially in the latter case, a great sense of expectation for a potential reward, whereas a reflexologist detects tension in your muscles with the help of micro-movement techniques. In a way, these physicians are able to tell that there is something going on with a particular organ based on the correlation they are trained to understand between a specific area and the internal tissue it's connected to. However, reflexology cannot diagnose or cure illnesses and those who practice it cannot prescribe medication in the same way general practitioners do. Although many trained experts may be tempted to act as medical doctors, they are not, nor should ever be perceived as such.

People who are unfamiliar with reflexology are also tempted to call it a glorified foot massage. Even though it is similar to a massage, a trained eye will be able to identify the fact that that a reflexologist does not manipulate soft tissue all over your body, but that he or she is targeting specific areas on the feet, hands or ears in accordance to a map of reflex points. This being said, there are portions of the Western medical community who genuinely seek to improve upon the way patients are treated. These individuals have committed to explore the benefits of reflexology in extremely thorough control studies, accounting for variables that range from publication bias to treatment consistency and quality and even the relative effect of the practice weighed against the subjective states of each individual.

Let's see what the results say. Centralized data on studies that go as far back as 1992 have shown that reflexology has a striking impact on fatigue and sleep disorders, as well as a noteworthy effect on general pain. Moreover, Denmark explored the effectiveness of reflexology in relation to employee stress levels and sick leave. Their reports consistently indicated relief in stress related conditions, as well as partial and even complete relief in the conditions where people sought the help of these practitioners. Almost 30% of all workers in one Danish district reported significantly higher levels of job satisfaction after 6 sessions with a trained and certified reflexologist, while their employers saved large amounts of money due to reduced sick leave. But Denmark is not the only nation to lead Western medicine towards this practice. Britons have also been outspoken in their desires to include complimentary alternative medicine (CAMs) free on the NHS. A one year survey ran by Therapy Director between 2012 and 2013 saw an overwhelming 92% of respondents say that they want more CAMs available in the national healthcare system. Quite at odds with the general opinion towards alternative medicine, another British study, conducted by YouGov in 2015, found that 49% of the participants firmly believe reflexology is helpful at curing illness.

By now, you're probably wondering what reflexology can do for you. As mentioned above, this fairly new practice provides powerful relief when it comes to stress and fatigue, while individuals suffering from sleep disorders have also reported significant improvement to their condition. But don't rush to close the book just yet. Scientists have also verified that reflexology is beneficial when dealing with PMS, headaches, diabetes, multiples sclerosis, cardiovascular issues, sinusitis, kidney function, anxiety, cancer treatment, overactive bladders and even dementia. The list seems pretty disparate, doesn't it? After all, these are quite a number of seemingly unrelated health concerns. However, when you consider the key organ systems that a certified reflexology professional can target through their massaging techniques, it all makes sense. It's also in accordance with the historical knowledge we have from this ancient practice.

So if it is beneficial, why isn't reflexology already implemented? Well, some researchers argue that reflexology has failed to demonstrate clinically effective results, but these *important* studies that are often quoted fail to account for the quality, length and full impact of the treatment on each subject. Consequently, a complex array of information is left out, such as the qualification of the therapist involved, the duration and value of the sessions or the patient's state before and after the treatment, which is why some of the most rigorous randomized control studies occur for periods of at least 6 months and require patients to keep extensive journals throughout this period. Given that reflexology is not yet a fully approved medical practice in Western medicine, it is understandable that some doctors might initially be hesitant towards its claims. Because it is so different from prescription medication, reflexology is yet to gain the institutional support it deserves.

However, while the majority of individuals are disbelieving towards reflexology, they shouldn't be blamed for their initial reluctance. Still, others kept an open mind and the numbers indicate that they were right to do so. Before we move on, there must be a mention on two other major advantages to reflexology you can benefit from, regardless of your illness, age or degree of belief in this practice. The first one relates to the fact that it is an alternative way, which means that it might help or even replace, *in some instances*, habits that are not even recommended by doctors. Brace yourself, we're stepping into the realm of drug side-effects. Those who deal with pain on a daily basis have to be weary of the consequences of the long-term usage of painkillers, whether they are NSAIDS, opioids or other, adjuvant, analgesics. NSAIDS (nonsteroidal anti-inflammatory drugs), for instance, are responsible for increased risk of stroke and heart attack, impaired kidney function and increased risk of bleeding. Opioids are known to affect hormone levels in our bodies, which means they can decrease the desire to have sex, induce fatigue, completely alter a woman's menstrual cycle or even cause galactorrhea – the secretion of breast milk in men or women who are not at a time when they are breast feeding. Other analgesics might include antidepressants or anticonvulsants, which are known to sedate and impair the cognitive functions of the patient.

This was just restricted example of a few types of medication prescribed to patients, as we speak, to help with their pain. Whether it's designed to lower cholesterol, manage insulin levels, calm your ache or otherwise, every drug has its own list of horrifying, *possible* side-effects. Take the time to read some of their incredibly long, incredibly small font prescription information. Do it carefully. Now, compare them to reflexology, which, when performed by a qualified, trained professional has absolutely none of these perplexing consequences. Suddenly, this alternative practice seems like an amazing idea. This doesn't mean you should completely disregard pharmaceuticals. Sometimes, they are necessary and our lives depend on them, but this doesn't have to be the status quo, since the *majority* of them do not treat the cause of your illness, but the symptoms.

And the last advantage reflexology offers you, as a patient, regardless of condition or age? The relationship *you develop* with the professional *you choose*. Once you've raised a disbelieving eyebrow, take a minute to consider what doctors and general practitioners do nowadays. They are instructed to find symptoms, construct a case and present you with the facts, as objectively as possible. Patients are not machines waiting for diagnostics software to give them results. Each and every one of them is a subjective entity with their own traits, life experience and aspirations. Simply put, patients are human beings who need emotional and psychological attention. Aside from the *fact* that our state of mind plays an important role in the healing process, reflexology offers you medical care beyond drugs, diagnostic sheets and associated symptoms. We often find it hard to translate these numbers into something that make sense for us. This is because the medical system is not prepared to deal with subjective entities, but rather with the illnesses that are common to them. Through reflexology, you are given a chance to relate to a person who *feels* your sickness, who *senses* your suffering and, because of the mutual relationship you develop, perceives your being as a whole.

Although intangible, this characteristic of reflexology drives a large number of previously unconvinced individuals to give this technique a chance. It's no wonder that a person capable of the simplest emotions might want a break from a community of scientific minds that constantly seeks to categorize and catalogue it, remove all of their *unique* features and completely disregard their idiosyncrasies. In a way, modern medicine de-personalizes all patient-doctor interaction. While it is true that a healthcare system is supposed to treat its patients fairly and equally throughout, which is the reason why objectivity is ideal, this is not always beneficial. For instance, it might help remove any bias one doctor might have towards a certain individual, but this would be counter-productive for reflexologists, who offer their services because of the *differences they share* with the people they treat. Modern medicine is supposed to be fast and effective, which is another consequence of the desire for objectivity. When you have template problems, you can offer template solutions. But human beings are not prototypes of the same model. In fact, our physiologies differ just as much as our characters do.

Especially when you are dealing with a chronic illness, it is important to increase the quality of life as much as possible. Imagine that you are a cancer patient. If you are not one, you can't accurately do it. Depending on the circumstance, it's not even ethical to do so. But, for the sake of this exercise, try to envision all of the difficulties and hardships you would have to undergo. Try to think of the things you enjoy doing the most and then imagine you can't do them anymore or, if you can, it's not the same. Now, bring your conscience into a state where it functions on a countdown timer. This is how much you have to live. Would you rather spend your remaining days under the influence of painkillers or enjoy significant relationships, moments and memories with other people? Obviously, you might not be able to deal with your condition without painkillers. However, if you consider that these reflexology sessions will contribute to your relaxation, help relieve pain, as well as reduce stress and anxiety, there is a considerable increase in the quality of life you are experiencing.

Chapter 3

Reflexology and its link to health, stress relief and weight loss

Reflexology has a strong impact upon the physical, emotional and psychological health of those who undergo regular sessions. Because there are so many questionable studies indicating the opposite, satisfied patients often agree to *share their experiences* to benefit other individuals suffering from a host of conditions and the side effects of medication that comes with them.

UK's Federation of Holistic Therapists regularly publishes such findings in their membership journal *International Therapist*. Intended primarily for professionals in complementary care, their publication sometimes features these cases as a way to connect the specific treatment of a particular person to certain outcomes.

Mrs. B, for instance, was a lady who didn't mind if people knew how reflexology helped her. As a 79 year old lady, she was suffering from sciatic pain, numbness in her left foot and intermittent buttock pain. She tried herbal remedies, physiotherapy, as well as acupuncture in her efforts to avoid regular pain medication as much as possible (nitrazepam, in her case). She also had bowel problems and bouts of anxiety.

After just two sessions, Mrs. B reported improved sleep and mobility. Following a conventional foot reflexology treatment that was combined with stimulation of nerve reflex points, she often felt the urge to go to the bathroom, whereas her pain improved significantly over the course of four weeks of treatment. On a visual analogue scale, her pain dropped from 8/10 to a 2/10, where 10 is the worst pain she ever felt and 0 was no pain. Most importantly, Mrs. B was able to walk a full mile without a helping stick, requiring only one short break. Her eating improved, along with her fluid intake and, even though her pain sometimes flared up, she was able to manage it significantly better than before, with minimal use of pharmaceuticals.

These are the facts from just one case, involving an elderly woman that was dealing with complex health issues. Her condition prevented her from leading a healthy life, turning even a walk on a sunny day into a horrid experience.

The facts are impressive, yes, but her confession that reflexology made her happy was beyond expression. Although her health concerns were not gone as a result of her reflexology sessions, she was able to manage them considerably better and find alternative ways to reduce her pain. But how did this happen? Is it something that anyone can try or was it just effective in her case? In order to make sense of such questions, we can take a closer look at some of the ways in which reflexology works upon our mind and body.

Although the body and the mind are not quite as distinct as we sometimes perceive them, for the sake of coherence, let's start with the impact of reflexology upon your body. The first thing you need to know is that this CAM (any CAM, for that matter) won't help you naturally and instantly shed 10, 20 or as many pounds as indicated by an advertisement. And it won't miraculously heal you either. That's just predatory advertising performed and condoned by people who do not uphold the ethical standard currently entertained by British reflexologists. Promoting such beliefs is unethical and harmful for you and every potential patient, as these false theories gradually become one's expectations. These initial, outlandish assertions will then be the cause of anxiety and other negative feelings, especially when one realizes that a few sessions with a professional did not confirm their expectations.

Let's see what the proverbial touch of a hand can and, in fact, really does in the context of a reflexology session. These practitioners believe that what they do heals you from within, so how does reflexology work within your body?

A good starting point is the lymphatic system. Part of the circulatory system, it plays a crucial role in our body's defence mechanism. The lymph, which is a clear, almost white fluid, has the purpose to carry bacteria and cancer cells from all over your body to your lymph nodes, located in the neck, armpit, groin and inside your chest and abdomen. In turn, these nodes filter the fluid and, if necessary, create white blood cells to fight off infections. This is why GPs often check the nodes under your neck, to see if they are swollen as a sign of infection. By stimulating lymphatic reflexes on the feet through an advanced technique that requires a certain amount of pressure, as well as specific movements, reflexologists de-congest your lymphatic system and encourage the natural drainage of the lymph. Individuals suffering from arthritis, fibromyalgia, headaches, migraines, chronic fatigue or ME, eczema, asthma, sinus problems, general aches or women with PMS have reported significant improvement in their condition as a result of reflexology lymph drainage (or RLD). Who would have thought that a touch can do so much?

The next best physiological change that reflexology brings about is an improvement in blood flow. The massage stimulates your circulatory system in a way that blood and oxygen circulates through your body more effectively, optimizing organ function and increasing your metabolism. Particularly if you're injured or sick and blood with fresh oxygen is needed somewhere in your body, these alternative medicine therapies will help you heal faster. With the help of fMRI readings, doctors ascertained that reflexology resulted in a considerable increase in blood flow to the kidneys and the intestines, improved kidney function when patients were on dialysis, lower blood pressure and anxiety as measured on EEGs and visibly reduced pain in a number of conditions including kidney stones, osteoarthritis, AIDS, etc.

Which brings us to our next point. When your digestive system is working appropriately and is sustained by a healthy metabolism, your body processes food more efficiently. Obviously, people who undergo reflexology will enjoy these benefits, but it doesn't mean that X pounds will be gone in a few weeks, not if other changes are not also implemented. If you consider some light exercise, varying your diet and eating healthy, then reflexology will give you an extra edge in the fight against excess weight.

Lastly, reflexology directly aids the opening and clearing of neural pathways by stimulating nerve endings in the feet. This is where it becomes obvious how this alternative technique can manage or completely eliminate pain. Like exercise or meditation, your body releases endorphins when the nerve terminations in your feet are stimulated. These endorphins act as natural pain killers and they can be so powerful that in some instances, pain is blocked altogether. What's more, our nervous system is easily overloaded. For some reason, it cannot handle multi-tasking, so it prioritizes. In instances of great pain, the treatment initially confuses the body as pain co-exists with endorphins and constant peripheral pressure. When it's too overwhelmed by endorphins, the nervous system gradually blocks out the pain, helping you relax.

By this time, we're beginning to realize just how complicated reflexology is. What started as something not that different from a Swedish massage is now shaping up to be a powerful healing tool we've been missing from our daily lives, a practice that can help us restore our physical and mental balance.

And speaking of mental poise, let's not forget that reflexology is just as valuable for your psyche as it is for your physiology. In our last example, reflexology worked on the body by altering the state of the central nervous system. We know these techniques help relieve and even eradicate pain and the example above shows a basic model of how this pain relief might occur. But there's more to it.

Based on the relationship that develops between patient and practitioner, reflexology has an intrinsic therapeutic side that helps us deal with psychological, behavioural and social issues. Starting from the fact that this therapy is centred on the subject, reflexology offers patients a kind of support they rarely benefit from, because modern day medical practice focuses on the disease, not the individual.

In order to speed up the healing process, doctors are instructed to find and deal with illnesses that are common to every person. On the other hand, reflexology therapists specifically look for how and where the symptoms manifest in your case. They do this because, in this practice, the healing is not directed towards the symptoms, but rather to what causes them.

Even modern medicine is changing its approach to take into account peoples' idiosyncrasies. Furthermore, just like our illnesses and the way our immune systems fight them off vary from one person to another, the way we see these afflictions also varies. This happens because every conscience has its own interpretation of reality. In a way, you could say that we live in completely different worlds and you wouldn't be wrong. Reflexology helps you focus on *your own views, feelings and concerns*, thus providing a framework to create a personal meaning from the circumstance you're in. Consequently, you'll be able to understand what is truly valuable for you and what isn't, acknowledge that your *body has its limitations* in terms of healing power, as well as energy. The latter should be directed towards the things that are important to you. Regardless of what they are – financial stability, interpersonal relationships, family, the sense of achievement from reaching a goal, etc. – this therapeutic relationship helps patients *realize* their true selves.

And the personal approach doesn't stop here. Possibly the most difficult part in dealing with illness is that it forces us to acknowledge the various paradoxes in our lives, the fact that not everything is logical or makes sense. For instance, pain, loss or death. Medical doctors might be able to prescribe you something that stops the physical ache for a while, but they rarely deal with the damage it does on our psyche and the havoc they wreak through our emotions, which is why reflexology is so effective when qualified professionals treat cancer patients. Even in controlled studies, the quality of life for cancer patients was greatly improved by reflexology. Beyond the physical benefits, they somehow *found a way to cope with their reality.* For healthy people, this might be unfathomable, but it's possible. The thing is that there's no pill that can do that for you.

Chapter 4

Myths about reflexology and common prejudices

Whenever an idea or a practice is new, people tend to form and propagate their own opinion about it. Some rely only on facts in their assessment, others use facts to a limited extent, while a few will completely disregard facts in an effort to transmit whatever it is they feel about the topic. It's also not uncommon for individuals to perceive new things as a threat to their way of life and reject them for that reason. For instance, people who claimed the Earth is round were ridiculed and even persecuted for centuries on end. Thankfully, now we know the surface of our planet is not flat, just like we know pennies dropped from skyscrapers are not deadly, although they will bruise you, or that milk is not *that* good for your bones, since there are more important factors that prevent them from receiving their necessary calcium.

"Zone therapy," as it was initially called by Dr William H. Fitzgerald in 1913 became reflexology in the 1930s and 1940s as a result of Eunice Ingham's research. It doesn't seem that new, does it? Still, an important part of the modern medical community and many scientists say otherwise. Technology gave us the possibility to observe via fMRI and EEGs the exact physiological impact of this CAM, proving beyond any shade of doubt its effectiveness on our mind and body. With this in mind, the myths often broadcasted by people who didn't have a chance to know the facts or who had an unpleasant experience with an unqualified therapist still have a definitive impact on the way we all perceive reflexology. Unsure what is real and what isn't? Here are a few common myths about reflexology.

Reflexology is a foot rub. This is the most common misconception about reflexology. Therapy sessions do starts off with a massage, but this has a strong purpose. Indeed, it is used to warm-up the skin of your soles and prepare the feet muscles for more complex movements. No lotion or cream is used and the only pieces of clothing you have to take off are your socks. That's it.

Reflexology is a pseudoscience based on placebo. This fable is particularly foretold among scientific circles. Whether they are true to their character or simply not aware of the facts, we can't tell. But here is something we do know. The Spanish Doctor Jesus Manzares conducted important research in the field. His extensive investigations actually identified deposits that are located in reflex areas of our feet – that's right, the very ones referred to as "crystals" by some traditional reflexologists. Entering the field of neurology, he explored these deposits and found that they contain nervous fibres and that they are, in fact, *associated with pain* and may differ in consistency based on the profoundness of the ache and its intensity. He also proposed reflexology protocols in dealing with these deposits, measuring exactly how much pressure, duration and frequency a therapist's moves must have in order to be beneficial in each case. Up to this date, his research spans almost three decades and over 70,000 clinical cases.

Of course, a placebo effect will always take place if you truly believe something will help you, regardless of what medical technique you're trying out. Think of it as your mind's way of lending your body a hand when it's supposed to heal itself. The tricky thing was separating the placebo impact from actual physiological signs. With the help of doctors such a Manzates, we can now say that these have been accurately pin-pointed. The data is out there, we just have to be willing to look for it.

Reflexology hurts. It's supposed to hurt, right? No pain, no gain… Wrong! Every single session you will have with a licensed therapist, a practitioner with at least 100 hours of training, is governed by two principles: *gentleness* and *communication*. Reflexologists are trained in the modulation of pressure. This doesn't mean that your reflexes can't be tender due to a number of reasons, like swelling and inflammation or deposits. If you're experiencing more than just pressure, you have to communicate to your therapist right then and there, to inform them what it is that you're feeling and they'll adjust. They won't mind and they will certainly not be offended. It's the other way around – they actually value your input as it gives them even more information and it allows them to *feel* more than their hands are able to tell them.

When you're in a lot of pain and even have some bruises to show for, you're definitely not in good (or maybe even qualified) hands. Which brings us to our next prejudice: **you're never going to jump straight on the table**. If you're looking for a quick foot-rub, reflexology might not be the best approach. Experienced professionals will require you to give them details about your lifestyle, current physical condition, as well as various issues and problems you've been suffering from. Basically, the therapist will want a medical history, but also to know you better, as a person and individual. Don't be surprised if they actually ask or care about what it is that you're expecting from your therapy sessions and what the ideal outcome for you looks like. Most practitioners are welcoming towards orthodox medicine or allopathic treatments, as they see reflexology working in a way that complements this approach. For this reason, you might even be asked to wait until they speak to your GP or the latter gives you the green light to undergo reflexology sessions.

As these techniques can impact a multitude of conditions and a great variety of organ systems or parts of your body, knowing you better helps the therapist ascertain what she or he needs to focus on during your sessions. If back pain is the usual forecast for you and you have to stand on your feet all day, there are specific modifications that can be made to the treatment to alleviate possible inflammation in the lumbar area and relax your muscles.

Speaking about pain, some people believe **needles are used during reflexology** sessions. Scary, yes, but it couldn't be further from the truth. Needles are used in *acupuncture and acupressure*, a completely different approach to the stimulation of points on our frame. The acupressure or acupuncture maps of our body do not always coincide with that of reflexology. But the biggest difference there is between the two is that acupressure employs over 800 reflex points along the meridians (thin energy lines) that span over the length of the entire human body, whereas reflexology focuses on your feet and hands.

At the end of the treatment, you'll always have a *closing discussion* about your experience and you'll receive more information about self-help techniques that will facilitate your body's healing. Whether it's taking it easy for the rest of the day, gentle exercise in the water, some diet adjustments, up your fluid intake or anything else, a reflexologist will always seek to give you health advice beyond what they manage to achieve during your sessions.

The last myth commonly entertained about reflexology is that it should **treat your disease**. This is a prejudice that stems from the way we view allopathic or conventional medicine. People are predisposed to the belief that prescriptions treat their diseases, when, in fact, these drugs deal with *the symptoms* emerging as a result of an illness.

It rarely happens that modern cures or doctors, for that matter, seek to solve the problem that caused the issue in the first place. Even with prescription pharmaceuticals, it is your body that performs the healing, not the pills you take. Sometimes, like in the case of viral infections (many sinus or ear infections and even the common flu and sore throat), antibiotics are completely useless. The fact is that antibiotics were developed to either kill or prevent bacteria from multiplying, not viruses. Against viruses, they can't do anything. Still, these pills are generously prescribed by doctors in case there may be a bacterial infection somewhere in the body, just in case.

Reflexology won't directly *treat* your disease, but you will *feel* better as a result of it and it will help your body *help itself*, initially and for the rest of the timeframe you choose to undergo this treatment. One way to view this therapy is as an additional boost, since reflexology can stimulate critical organ systems in your body to work better, improve lymph drainage, as well as blood flow. In turn, these will facilitate your healing and alleviate your pain and stress (or completely eradicate them). This is why reflexology was proven to be effective for the people who deal with asthma or sinus infections, where common medicine doesn't do much. Practitioners refer to it as a deep stimulation of your musculo-skeletal system, which puts your mind into a state of relaxation. During the process, your body can attain homeostasis and heal itself faster or recover successfully from diseases or fatigue.

These are only some of the most common myths you'll encounter about reflexology. Although they may seem tempting, the scientific proof in favour of the effectiveness of reflexology can help you shatter the fiction and shed light on *what actually happens* during a treatment session. To avoid any unpleasant experience, always make sure that you check the accreditation of the practitioner, regardless of recommendation. If the reflexologist is qualified, they should be able to provide credentials, as well as uphold certain standards in terms of cleanliness, professionalism and client care. Whenever you're uncertain, don't hesitate to seek the advice of your local reflexology associations, as they will be able to give you an informed opinion.

Chapter 5

A brief history of reflexology

We owe the term reflexology to Vladimir Bekhterev, a Russian neurologist who was particularly known for his study of human reflexes. In 1907, he published the book that would later define him as one of the founders of objective psychology. In the meantime, he also coined the term "reflexology". Although he did come up with the designation, the way Bekhterev understood this practice is inconceivable to a modern reflexologist. He thought of these techniques as a way to examine the human being from an **objective perspective**, one that relied solely on what we all have in common from a biological, as well as social standpoint. This is not a hermit's belief, but rather an idea that was immensely popular in Western medical practice and, to a great extent, still is. It serves as proof for the fact that reflexology as a complimentary practice must have its roots elsewhere. As Westerners, we did not invent it, but we did make valuable and important contributions to it. In a way, without this cultural (mis)appropriation of reflexology, it's likely that the latter would never have been acknowledged for its full potential and benefits. Quite ironic, isn't it?

But let's not get ahead of ourselves. In order to highlight the origins of reflexology, let's take a closer look at how it developed within our Occidental culture since colonial times, when it was first mentioned. Starting with the 14th century, Europe began trading with the Orient more frequently and in larger amounts of goods. However, people brought home not just merchandise, but unusual traditions, novel ideas and knowledge of entirely different cultures, human behaviours and lifestyles; or rather, their opinion of what was witnessed in these far-away lands. The earliest known Western treatise on reflexology, then called zone therapy, dates back to 1582 and was published in Europe by Dr. Adamus and Dr. A'tatis.

A few centuries later, the American Dr. Fitzgerald becomes the father of modern reflexology, as he is often referred to today. An Ear, Nose and Throat specialist on active duty at the Boston City Hospital, he managed to publish his work on zone therapy in 1917. In it, he wrote about ten vertical zones (very similar to the 12 meridians in traditional Chinese medicine or TCM) that extend throughout the length of the human body and discovered that when pressure was applied to certain points on the body, pain would either cease for that duration or go away entirely. He *did not give any official credit* to where his ideas came from, although he studied and worked in Vienna at the turn of the century, when the German-speaking world was already investigating "reflex massage" techniques. He was also a trained physician, which rendered his claims more trustworthy, thus compelling others to regard them seriously.

The fact of the matter is that the European **scientific community was already highly preoccupied with the subject matter** of reflexes before Fitzgerald published anything. In other words, a heavy context inspired his writings and findings. In the 1890s, Sir Henry Head effectively laid the terrain for this discipline to grow by proving that there is an undeniable connection between our internal organs and the skin, a link which is facilitated by nervous system. In 1902, the German doctor Alfons Cornelius published a treatise on pressure points, confirming that there are certain spots on our body that incite physiological changes when one applies force on them. Just two years later, Pavlov won the Nobel Prize for his discovery of the conditioned reflex response. And this is just what was happening in Europe around the time when Fitzgerald was visiting Vienna. Although Fitzgerald was still working with the 10 vertical divisions of the human body that are quite familiar to TCM, he was the one who really brought zone therapy to the spotlight. His greatest impact would be to train and work with Dr. Joe Shelby Riley, who further expounded on Fitzgerald's assumptions, created the first diagrams of reflex areas located on our feet and, possibly the most important aspect, met with the person that some consider the *true* "father" of modern day reflexology… or mother.

Eunice Ingham started working with Dr. Riley in 1919. Ingham began developing her own theories of pressure points around 1930 based on her experience with patients, as well as Dr. Riley's diagrams. In 1938, she published her first book on reflexology, called "Stories the feet can tell". In her long-lasting career, she would publish another two books on the subject. Albeit less scientific, Ingham's contributions were significant, which is why she was encouraged by Riley to take her research to the wide public or those who would benefit the most from these techniques. Because she was not a qualified, trained physician, her claims were not regarded with the same degree of authority as Fitzgerald's. The fact that she was also a woman in a field where men were considered specialists didn't help. So her only hope was to listen to Riley and reach out to the non-medical community. This is possibly the reason why she was afraid to use the term "reflexology" and opted for "compression reflex massage" instead, even though it was obvious that she did not believe reflexology to be a branch of massage therapy.

In retrospect, this was a very subtle and intelligent approach, as her voice might have turned others away from reflexology, despite her being right about what she was saying. Therefore, Eunice Ingham avoided negative feedback and consistently improved the techniques that she learned from Dr. Riley. More importantly, if Dr. Fitzgerald believed that pressure can **numb the pain** by providing the nervous system with a stimulus which overrides it, Ingham was of the opinion that the alternation of pressure stimulates our body to **heal better and faster**. One could say that she is *responsible* for the fact that we think of reflexology nowadays as a healing practice, rather than a painkiller. At this point, we do not only believe what Eunice Ingham said, but we've also managed to prove that she was right.

Around the time when she was still conceptualizing what was to be *the first detailed map of the reflex area of the feet*, Dr. Charles Sherrington made another discovery that would change the way scientists regard reflexology. In his attempts to prove that Pavlov wasn't exactly right when he postulated that there is a direct and simple relationship between stimulus and response, Sherrington demonstrated that the response is, in fact, dependent on the nerve itself, not the size of the stimulus. For instance, a small nerve couldn't send a bigger signal to the brain than its capacity allowed, whether the stimulus was exactly as much as it can handle or ten times stronger. What's more, Sherrington coined the term **proprioception** or the body's ability to sense internal stimuli regardless of ability to see. Even if we're blindfolded, we can tell whether our leg is straight, slightly off the ground or bent at the knee. For reflexology, this meant that a small amount of force can be just as effective in stimulating a pressure area, but also that the nervous and muscular systems of the human anatomy are interwoven and that when we work with the muscles, we're also working with the brain. His contributions to the science community earned Sherrington the Nobel Prize in 1932. Since then, the available technology and neurologists have also told us that proprioception is idiosyncratic – unique to each individual and dependent on their personal experiences, health and physiology.

In the following decades, through the interest of some doctors, as well as the overwhelming desire in many patients to try alternative cures, this complimentary alternative medicine spread and gained its very own foundation in our culture. In 1969 reflexology was the subject matter of arguably the first successful self-help book ever published, Mildred Carter's *Helping Yourself with Reflexology*. Great Britain saw the advent of reflexology because of Eunice Ingham. Indeed, it was one of her students, Doreen Bayly, who brought her discoveries back to the UK in the 1960.

So what of the **ancient heritage**? We understand reflexology today in completely different terms than we did at the beginning of the 20th century, but our conclusions are very much in the spirit of the Eastern philosophy, where these ideas first originated. Whether it was Egypt 2450 BC, China 3000 BC, the Inca civilization or various practices used by Native Americans, there are strong cultural traditions that connect the sense of touch to our health. Spanning different areas of the globe and using entirely separate systems of belief to explain what's going on, there is a whole philosophy of healing at the foundation of reflexology.

If you didn't have MRI or EEG scanners to tell you that your brain waves have changed as a result of these pressure points being stimulated, wouldn't it make sense to explain your feeling better as a result of a complicated reflex therapy in a more metaphorical way? "Prana" for the Indians or "Qi/Chi" for the Chinese is such a way to describe the benefits of massaging one's feet. The relationship that a healer develops with their patient can be described as an energy transfer, if you look at it from the perspective that one individual invests their being into the task of healing another. However, this therapeutic exchange becomes an obsolete system if all patients are treated speedily, as if they have the same illness that can be cured in the same way. The desire for increased efficiency has minimized *human* contact and rendered the entire process superficial and sterile of emotion.

For this reason, before there was any institutionalized way to accredit practitioners of reflexology, many tried to stay true to its origins, while adapting its techniques to their own culture. Consequently, therapists tried to translate phenomena like prana or qi into more familiar ideas such as "vital energy" or "life force".

Many patients do claim they have found their vital energy after such sessions, whether it was because of stress relief, ability to cope with pain better or a sense of inner balance. To an extent, the fact that the scope of zone therapy was secularized, brought from the spiritual dimension of the East into the strictly material, physical one of the West was a trial that proved its worth. After surviving this transfer and translation, reflexology gained even more awareness with the general public and it evolved into the practice that we know today.

Chapter 6

How does reflexology actually work?

Some of you might have skipped directly to this chapter for a quick answer to the title. That's alright. However, if you've been reading up to this point, you already have a strong understanding of what reflexologists do or... don't do, how their techniques are supposed to affect our bodies and the folklore that's been created around this fairly new complimentary alternative medicine. So, let's not disappoint those of you who are hungry for facts, particularly since knowing how reflexology works will help you develop a healthy attitude towards this practice and dispel lingering prejudices about it. Prepare your mind for a short and simple incursion into basic neurology, a summary of what (usually) happens during a session, as well as a description of the physiological, psychological and emotional consequences of a session. Basically, we'll see just how reflexology works throughout your body, in your mind and with your emotions.

So what **does reflexology** do? One way to answer this question is by explaining its physical effects. The most widespread form of reflexology focuses on the foot and the ankle. Physiologically speaking, our feet contain over 7000 nerve endings, 19 muscles and 107 ligaments connecting 26 bones. Now, reflexologists and supporters of this CAM keep saying that the entire human body is represented on the soles of our feet, but is that *accurate*?

Yes it is. How do we know? Well, in neurology terms, what a reflexologist does can be seen as the stimulus part of a reflex arc. It all starts with the *sensory receptors* in your skin. When the therapist so much as touches your skin, the receptors or nerve endings in that particular area send an instant impulse straight to your central nervous system or CNS. The first part of the nervous system that receives the impulse is your spinal cord, which regulates all of the involuntary reflexes; for instance, how fast your heart is beating or even your breathing.

Most of the time we're not aware of our breathing, nor are we controlling it, but someone has to do it and that's the spine. Now, you can say that the reason stimuli are first processed in the spine and then go to the brain is a protection mechanism. Of course, the spine doesn't really "think", but there's a reason why it is far simpler than our cortex and most of what it does is just react. The fact the spine's grey matter is structured in a less complicated manner than that in our brain makes it incredibly fast in determining what signal to send back to the area that is stimulated. This is why the withdrawal reflex (nociceptive) is located in the spine. If you feel pain, in around 0.5 seconds you'll involuntarily flex your muscle to pull the injured part. As you may have already noticed, you start pulling away even before you literally feel the pain, which further proves the efficiency of our CNS. Makes sense.

In addition, the signal travels to the **reticular formations of the brain** after the reflex was initiated, so that we may further analyse what took place. Not coincidentally, the very same network of nerve pathways governs other bodily functions that are essential to our survival, such as pain modulation, sleep, cardiovascular control or our ability to move. Luckily, science has allowed us to understand the reticular formations of the brain. Today, we know that they hold a *representation of the human body* that links each and every area of our physiology to specific points in the brain. Neurologists understand reflexology in these terms and some of them strive to improve its non-invasive techniques by analysing the zones on our feet that generate the maximum **bio-electric response** within the reticular formations.

You can also think of the brain as a system that is constantly providing feedback to you based on what it is feeling. Imagine, for a second, that you're your very own brain, telling yourself that you're in constant pain and that something needs to be done. You don't really care what and, quite possibly, you don't know how to ameliorate the pain. If there are no signs of improvement, you're already envisioning hell for the rest of your life, so you start screaming at your consciousness: Do something! In that moment of agony, when you often feel that nobody can understand what you're going through, reflexology sends you a signal from the feet that is different from that of pain, stiffness or discomfort. Initially, you're *speechless*, but then you start to gain perspective on what's going on, understand your situation and divert energy to improve the healing in that area. This is why reflexology *doesn't cure*, but **helps you cure** yourself, because its impact is rivalled by few other practices. In other words, it offers a desperately needed re-calibration and relief for your central nervous system. Afterwards, the brain starts to relay these positive signals to the organ systems associated with areas stimulated by the therapist, which is the reason why most people stop feeling pain altogether, while others experience a sense of relief.

Moreover, reflexology has a significant impact upon the baroreceptor reflex via the central nervous system. The former is a homeostatic mechanism, and therefore a process that is essential to our survival, because it ensures an inner balance in the physiological and psychological functions of our body. If our body cannot achieve homeostasis, we initially get sick and, if this persists, we die. That's how vital balance is for our system. Within the larger frame of human homeostasis, the *baroreflex regulates blood pressure* by acting opposite to its current levels in an attempt to stabilize our system. As an example, when you're hypertensive (your blood pressure is high) this reflex has the responsibility to tell your heart to slow down, which, in turn, decreases cardiovascular tension. Practically speaking, this means that reflexology is very beneficial for individuals who experience blood pressure problems, as well as for those who suffer from an illness in general. When the reflexologist operates with techniques that help the patient relax and achieve homeostasis with greater ease, they are effectively speeding up the healing process, allowing the organism to divert the resources it would otherwise spend on achieving this tricky balance to making you feel better, repairing injuries or killing foreign organisms.

So far, this is some of the theory behind reflexology. But **what exactly takes place during a session** of reflexology? In a previous section, we've dealt with what some people *think* about reflexology and even what others have experienced under the hands of unqualified professionals who mistakenly call themselves reflexologists. In order to make things easier and get you more accustomed with what's supposed to happen during a session with a certified practitioner, we'll lay out a sketch of a first meeting.

It's vital that you're aware of the fact that **communication** is essential to this process. Unlike ordinary medicine, an efficient reflexology session is, actually, based on the feedback you provide to your practitioner – so *be ready to talk* and voice what your feelings and emotions. This also includes whatever questions you may have about them or what they will be doing. If, for any reason, a professional is dismissive with your inquiries or avoids them, you have every reason to terminate the session.

Before anything happens, the practitioner will ask you to provide a medical history, focusing on your ailments and physical concerns. To the degree that you are comfortable with this, you can also share psychological or emotional details, as this will help your specialist estimate the level of stress you're currently dealing with. Depending on your condition, they might advise working just on the feet or the hands. In some rare instances, it's also possible that *they will refuse to treat* you, because the stimulating effect of reflexology on your circulation might worsen your condition. But this is only valid if you suffer from DVT (deep vein thrombosis), blood clots or phlebitis/thrombophlebitis. Similarly, if you suffer from any serious medical conditions, a qualified reflexologist will not treat you unless they also receive a green light from your general practitioner.

Medical history out of the way, the reflexologist will proceed to assess the soles of your feet for bunions, sores, rashes or plantar warts. You should also be ready for them to either wash your feet or ask you to do so in a designated area and then soak them in warm water for a short time.

Afterwards, you'll either sit or lie down in a comfortable position. Based on the information you've previously given, the reflexologist already has a good idea of what they need to focus on. During the time they prepare your feet, their opinion will be seconded by the signs (tension, deposits, swelling, etc.) in specific areas of your soles. They will literally **feel** your pain, along with its intensity and consequences. These signs are caused either by a local condition or by the nervous inputs transmitted from the reticular formations of the brain to the associated areas on your soles.

As a general rule, no lotions are used, but a moisturizing cream might be required for thickened skin or if your soles are very dry. Dryness promotes friction, which is never a pleasant experience, so a bit of cream sometimes works wonders to reduce discomfort. Even if the therapist will say that specific pressure points need a lot of attention, they will still work the entire area of the foot in order to help the entire body achieve homeostasis and even out the energy flow. If you have a tender area and the practitioner applies a bit too much pressure, **you must say so**. Regardless of what you think, this is helpful. They won't be offended or disregard what you are saying. If they do so, you should consider terminating the session. Typically, congestions are dealt with using restraint and care. The reflexologist will apply just enough pressure to provoke a stimulus to a certain reflex point, or sometimes to *work it*, but not so much as to cause pain or serious discomfort. The pain usually subsides because the nervous system is stimulated in the right manner and the body starts to heal itself better, while your psyche is relieved by unnecessary stress. It's likely that you may experience a variety of odd sensations, at a physical, psychological and even emotional level, such as light-headedness, deep sighing, increased energy, tiredness or even crying. Nonetheless, such reactions are an indication that your body is returning to a state of balance. Most of the time, your body will be experiencing overwhelmingly **positive signs**.

At the end of the session, the therapist will adjust their technique so as to make the transition from that state of relaxation easier. You shouldn't be surprised if they give you diet tips to follow, recommendations about activities for the rest of the day or small movements you can do on your own. Even if it's not what you usually do, follow these steps and you'll be surprised to see that you can also help your body heal better over time.

Chapter 7

Reflexology diagram reference

As you've already guessed, this chapter is dedicated to reflexology diagrams of the feet and hands. But why talk about diagrams at all? Well, this will help you *see* the way a reflexologist looks at your body. The first valuable piece of information you'll take away from your first session is that everything within us is connected. We are a result of the harmony (or lack of) that exists between the multitude of organ systems working together within our bodies.

We are also a result of the consonance that exists between our body and the lifestyle we put it through, whether it involves staying indoors for 20 hours a day, eating junk food at breakfast and dinner, relying on pharmaceuticals to cure us or exercising every day. Just like we've stopped looking at bloodletting as a viable means to treat a wide range of diseases, it's necessary that we acknowledge the connections that exist inside and outside of ourselves for what they truly are.

These maps will come in handy especially if you're interested in trying out some basic routines on your own. In Chapter 8 and 9, you'll find advice on how you can use the diagrams to help with some common or complex conditions we all face at one point or another.

If you're wondering where these **diagrams came from**, the charts we rely on today are a result of the pioneering work conducted by physical therapist Eunice Ingham. Trained by Dr. Shelby Riley, she was also familiar with Dr. Fitzgerald's Zone Therapy. Since then, her work has been continuously refined and tweaked by various researchers and scientists looking to prove reflexology right. Their patient studies are also verified thorough feedback from the field of neurology. The latter helped us understand the *connection* between our feet and various organ systems. Given our current familiarity with the human brain, we now know that the nervous impulse determined by the practitioner's intervention is sent to the reticular formations in our brain, an area that actually connects the cerebrum, cerebellum and spinal cord. And then there's the fact that these formations hold a point-by-point map of each physiological area within us. Now let's see get to it!

Foot Charts

Plantar View

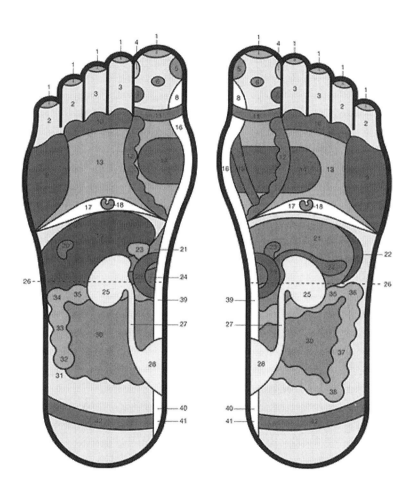

Dorsal view

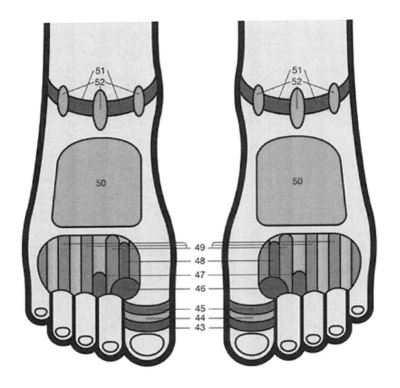

Lateral view

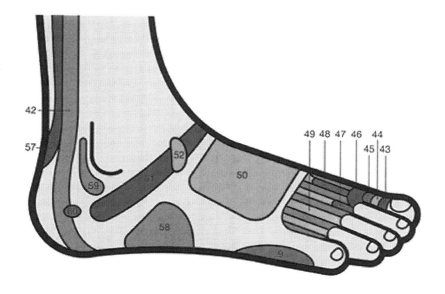

Medial View

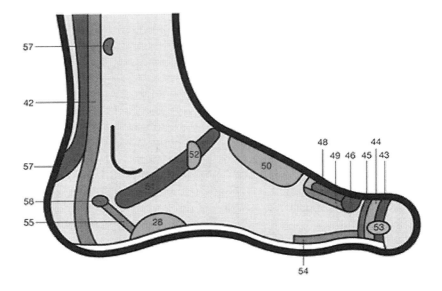

Foot Charts Reference:

1. Brain

2. Sinuses/Outer Ear

3. Sinuses/Inner Ear/Eye

4. Temple

5. Pineal/Hypothalamus

6. Pituitary

7. Side of Neck

8. Cervical Spine

9. Shoulder/Arm

10. Neck/Helper to Eye, Inner Ear, Eustachian Tube

11. Neck/Thyroid/Parathyroid/Tonsils

12. Bronchial/Thyroid Helper

13. Chest/Lung

14. Heart

15. Oesophagus

16. Thoracic Spine

17. Diaphragm

18. Solar Plexus

19. Liver

20. Gallbladder

21. Stomach

22. Spleen

23. Adrenals

24. Pancreas

25. Kidneys

26. Waist Line

27. Ureter Tube

28. Bladder

29. Duodenum

30. Small Intestine

31. Appendix

32. Ileocecal Valve

33. Ascending Colon

34. Hepatic Flexure

35. Transverse Colon

36. Splenic Flexure

37. Descending Colon

38. Sigmoid Colon

39. Lumbar Spine

40. Sacral Spine

41. Coccyx

42. Sciatic Nerve

43. Upper Jaw/Teeth/Gums

44. Lower Jaw/Teeth/Gums

45. Neck/Throat/Tonsils/Thyroid/Parathyroid

46. Vocal Cords

47. Inner Ear

48. Lymph/Breast/Chest

49. Chest/Breast/Mammary Glands

50. Mid-Back

51. Fallopian Tube/Vas Deferens/Seminal Vesicle

52. Lymph/Groin

53. Nose

54. Thymus

55. Penis/Vagina

56. Uterus/Prostate

57. Chronic Area-Reproductive/Rectum

58. Leg/Knee/Hip/Lower Back Helper

59. Hip/Sciatic

60. Ovary/Testes

Plantar foot aspect

This diagram represents your feet soles or their underside. Of all the areas on our body, the soles are the ones that contain **the most pressure points**, which is why they benefit from so much attention. It's also the area of our body that facilitates (or facilitated) a great part of our connection to the environment, a link that is now completely transformed by footwear. What we're missing out on because of our shoes is *grounding,* the physical process that charges us with negative electrons. Grounding has numerous benefits on human physiology via the nervous system, which is why it feels so comforting to sometimes walk barefoot on sand, grass or even cold earth.

Dorsal foot aspect

The dorsal side of the foot is a map of the later from the perspective you have when you look down. Few people are aware of the fact that our feet are the area in the human body that contains the second most density in terms of bones – 26 (a hand has 27). When any of these bones is out of alignment, our entire body deviates from the normal posture.

Lateral foot aspect

As the name suggests, this is the outside edge of the foot or the area that's most likely to hurt when you sprain your ankle.

Medial foot aspect

The medial aspect or the inside edge runs from your big toe to your heel. It's also the one where your arch is. Anatomically speaking, the foot actually has three arches, each of them maintained by a set of bones. The role of these arches is to absorb the forces that our feet have to endure on a day-to-day basis in such a manner that a fraction of the impact is actually felt throughout the upper leg. Up to 30% of people do not develop one arch, a condition that's called flat feet and which changes the biomechanics of the leg entirely.

What the foot *feels* like in a particular pressure point gives information to your practitioner about the health issues you currently experience or that you might have had in your past. It's not because of a sixth sense, but rather because our body has a memory of its own when it comes to serious or severe illnesses and it remembers them. This memory often translates into a sensitive reflex. Still, a reflexologist cannot diagnose an illness in the same way your GP can, a limit which every qualified reflexologist thoroughly acknowledges and respects.

Hand Chart (overleaf)

LEFT PALM

RIGHT PALM

1. Head skull
2. Frontal sinuses
3. Epiphysis
4. Pituitary
5. Nape
6. Face
7. Nose
8. Eyes
9. Ears
10. Trapeze
11. Shoulder, wrist
12. Arm
13. Knee, elbow
14. Leg
15. Ankle
16. Lungs, bronchi
17. Stomach
18. Duodenum
19. Pancreas
20. Liver

21. Gallbladder
22. Small intestine
23. Appendix
24. Ileum
25. Ascending colon
26. Trasverse colon
27. Discending colon
28. Rectum
29. Anus
30. Kidney
31. Ureter
32. Bladder
33. Heart
34. Spleen
35. Thyroid
36. Cervical vertebrae
37. Dorsal vertebrae
38. Lumbar vertebrae
39. Ovaries
40. Uterus, prostate

The diagram on the previous page gives a palmar aspect of each hand. An important advantage of hand reflexology is that the hands are closer to your spinal cord than your feet, which means that you'll feel the benefit of a routine much faster than in the case of feet. Babies are privileged with two hand reflexes that are lost in adulthood, namely the grasping reflex and the Babkin reflex. These are evolutionary mechanisms that help the baby grasp objects when they touch them with their hand (in the first case) or stimulate the breast for a better flow while breastfeeding (in the second). It's also very common for babies to eagerly open their mouth and turn their head in anticipation of goodies coming their way, so next time you apply pressure to both hands of a baby, think of the Babkin reflex.

Hand reflexology is often recommended by practitioners as a way to help our bodies between sessions or when we want to cope with a great deal of pain. You can work on the hands yourself without asking anybody to help out. The reflexologist can show you the exact movements and the exact places where they must be done. A big bonus is that you don't have to take off your shoes or socks to work on your hands, which would be pretty awkward if you were out on a date, at a family reunion or in a meeting at the office. Touching one's hands is also a socially acceptable practice that goes unnoticed, most of the times. Consequently, nobody has to know that you're in pain or having issues if you don't want them to. And hands do play their part in non-verbal communication, so you might want to be more descriptive in conversations if you plan to not use your hands on purpose.

All in all, this chapter was meant to get you more acquainted with the way a reflexologist looks at your feet and hands. Besides everything we've mentioned, these professionals have working medical knowledge of the human anatomy that is comparable to that of any medical doctor. They are able to give sound nutritional advice and lifestyle suggestions that will complement your treatment and facilitate a better healing on your part. On the other hand, reflexologists do not regard illnesses in the same manner palliative medicine does, nor do they possess the diagnosing skills that a GP does. Even if your practitioner has enough experience to be able to *tell* what your health concerns are, they will never go as far as issuing a medical diagnosis, as this goes against the ethics of practice that they uphold. In the next chapter, we'll put these diagrams to good use and give you a sample of what reflexology *feels* like. For some of you, these routines might prove to be highly beneficial and helpful in providing some much-needed relief without involving chemicals or resorting to invasive procedures.

Chapter 8

Practicing reflexology

In this chapter, you'll find a few basic movements that can help alleviate the discomfort, pain and stress caused by some of the most common aches we're likely to experience: something easy to do and very practical that you can take with you from our brief incursion into reflexology. Applied with care, these basic movements will be very useful and will open up the world of reflexology for you and your family.

Following the areas indicated on the foot or the hand diagram, you may use the described techniques to find your balance between sessions or as a sample of what reflexology can do for you. Please note that, if they are not performed by a qualified professional, they are likely not to have the same impact or efficiency in helping you out. What's more, you **must** be highly observant of your *reactions and symptoms* when performing these movements and cease immediately if there's any sign that you're experiencing bad side-effects or if your symptoms are getting worse.

With this in mind, we've tried to direct our attention to a list of incredibly common problems, some of which we're all bound to experience at one point or another during our lives. These include: migraines, neck and back pain, shoulder pain, anxiety, stress and tension, sciatica and sleep difficulties.

Before you try anything out, though, take a few minutes to examine the feet and hand diagrams described in the previous chapter. They have a history of their own and, even as we speak, scientists keep improving upon which tiny points might be better than others for a particular organ system. Nevertheless, even if there is continuous evolution, a standard and a general consensus allow professionals to interact and discuss the subject of pressure points on a daily basis. For instance, it's highly unlikely that a qualified reflexologist will target your pituitary and adrenal glands by working your heel. In addition, a practitioner might come to the conclusion that other systems in your body need the same amount of attention in order for it to be able to heal itself properly. Don't forget that, if you have any questions, you should feel at ease to ask them.

Some techniques also involve working pressure points that are either on the sides or the front of your hands/feet, so you shouldn't feel anxious if your therapist involves these areas as well. If you'd like to try this yourself, you should give the routines a go for a couple of days and jot down your feelings and symptoms, for accuracy.

Sleep issues (diagram reference feet – adrenal glands)

The adrenal glands are the ones most responsible for our sleeping patterns, which is why this routine is meant to stimulate the hypothalamus, pineal and pituitary. Locate the **centre of your toe** with your finger, then *slide* your finger up towards the tip, *rotate* a few times and repeat. This is a very basic movement benefitting the hypothalamus and the pineal glands.

For the pituitary, perform the same sliding motion to the lateral side of your toe. This reflex point you should be able to identify as a small pea. Try not to use too much pressure, but enough of it to feel something. Perform these motions for at least 1 minute each on both of your toes.

In addition, your practitioner may pay attention to your liver and lymphatics during this routine, as detoxing and the immune system are also vital for a restful sleep.

Migraines (diagram reference feet and hands – head and brain areas)

If you're struggling with migraines, working the areas associated with the brain and head might prove very helpful. These are located on the **top edge of the dorsal part of your toes**. Using your index finger, perform a sliding motion on the outer edge of your toes, starting with the big toe and going all the way down to the small one. You can alternate this motion with the finger walking or biting technique – instead of sliding, you move by *flexing the joint* right above your hand finger's nail. Then, massage the same reflex points on your hand fingers. These are located **close to the joint, at the bottom of your fingerprints** (no. 1 on the chart).

Reflexologists will also focus on the neck and back, as tension from these areas usually radiates to the brain and amplifies or even causes headaches.

Back pains (diagram reference feet and hands – back areas)

Heavy lifters or people who have to stand up a lot are almost certain to have some back pains during the day. To relieve it, start with a sliding movement on the **side of your foot right** from the tip of your toe and go down until the heel. Repeat a few times and then again with finger walking. You can then shift to horizontal finger walking on **your arch**. You start from right underneath your big toe mound and slowly go sideways until you can feel your bone. Repeat by going down in small increments until you reach your heel. In addition, you may locate a bony prominence on the exterior side of your heel, right underneath your ankle. The points around it are responsible for the knee, hip and lower back areas. Right **after the prominence**, towards your heel, is the lower back area. You start in bites from above the prominence, go over it into the lower back area and then rotate back.

Last, but not least, you can work the lower back, pelvis and the sacroiliac joints by starting from the prominence and going **down towards your heel** in small bites. When you reach the end, turn back and move your finger slightly higher than your previous trajectory until you reach1 cm or so under the ankle. If you're at work or in a place where you can't just start massaging your feet, massaging your hands can also provide relief for your back pain. All you have to do is slide and/or finger-walk the right area on the side of your thumb (no. 36, 37 and 38 on the hand diagram).

Neck pains (diagram reference feet and hands – neck areas)
Neck pains go hand in hand with desk jobs. Luckily, you can help relieve them by massaging the **neck area on the joint of your big toe**, as indicated by the diagram. You can also complement this reflex point with the head area on your other toes and the shoulder area, underneath your small toe. Again, you can use both sliding and finger-walking.

On your hand, the neck corresponds to the **area right underneath your thumb joint** (no. 5 on the chart). Many people are not aware of the fact that tension from your neck greatly contributes to headaches, so combining these areas with the head ones will prove even more effective in dealing with migraines without pharmaceuticals.

Anxiety and stress relief (diagram reference feet and hands – heart, lungs and thyroid)

Are you constantly pressed by overcrowded schedules, tough decisions at work and a busy family life? You're in need of an essential relief from anxiety and stress. The hectic lifestyle of the 21st century often takes a toll on our systems, which means that our bodies tend to lag behind in terms of recovery. Not getting enough sleep, the necessary nutrients or even enough water further complicates things. The danger is that an incomplete recovery puts even more strain on our physiology, often translating into constant fatigue, more sleep issues (now you actually want to sleep, but you can't) and even a weakened immune system.

In order to facilitate a faster and more efficient recovery, we can get rid of our anxiety and stress through reflexology. To do this, work the heart and lung areas, using the two basic movements we've learned so far. The increased oxygenation from the lungs synergizes with the improved circulation from your heart. This routine will calm you down and prepare your body to enter homeostasis faster. After a few good minutes, you should move on to the thyroid pressure area, which starts right between your big toe and your next finger. One of the benefits of working the thyroid area is that this will greatly decrease muscle tension. If anxiety is more concerning for you and you still feel jittery, you should move on to the solar plexus point, roughly 2 centimetres down on your sole, right between your second and third toe.

If you can't work on your feet, you can massage the following areas on the hand chart: lung (no. 16), heart (no. 33) and thyroid (no. 35).

Stomach aches and digestion problems (diagram reference feet and hands – stomach and pancreas, colon, small intestine)

Stomach issues have become so common after large meals that pharmaceutical companies tend to double or even triple their TV ads during the holidays. But what if you could cope with that pain or even make it disappear altogether, without the use of drugs? To give it a try, use the two techniques we've discussed on the following points of your feet: stomach and pancreas (starting from the inside of your foot and working your way towards the arch), the colon (starting from the outside, working your way towards the inside of the foot, down then towards the exterior again) and the small intestine (working from the inside out and descending on a lower path in small increments). If you're still at the table, then you can discreetly work numbers 17, 22, 25, 26 and 27 on your hand.

All of these techniques are also employed by reflexologists. However, they improve upon them through other methods far more advanced, as well as by working other related systems to increase the efficiency of the treatment. The idea is not to learn either of the charts or movements by heart, but rather to familiarize yourself with a few basic techniques that might save you a lot of headache (even literally) in the long run. By consulting the book, try to do one of the routines that you think would help you the most. In no less than a few days of doing it daily, you won't even need the chart to know where you need to press.

Just remember! It is imperative that you exercise caution when performing any of these routines and that you try to keep an open mind. Be consistent for a period of time and take notes of any improvements/side-effects you might be feeling. It often happens that practitioners themselves recommend small sequences to help you out between sessions, so you might turn back to these charts even after your first session with a practitioner. Even if these movements prove to be highly effective, nothing we can describe here will fully replace the benefits of an entire session or the touch of a professional with extensive knowledge of this practice.

Chapter 9

Advanced techniques

So far, we've used reflexology to treat a number of very common complaints, such as headache or back pain. To this end, we've learned about basic reflexology techniques that involved walking and making circles on or around the reflex areas concerned.

However, reflexology can be used to speed up the healing process even with complicated conditions, such as acne, asthma, irritable bowel syndrome and more. Although we cannot fully explore in our brief summary the complex movements a qualified reflexologist will use in order to alleviate these disorders, we can take a look at some of the most widespread advanced techniques used in such instances.

If you are curious about their effects or if your reflexologist recommended them to you in between sessions, feel free to try these movements out on your own. Always remember, however, that in order to achieve the best results, you should consult an experienced practitioner who can better guide you through your body's healing process. Also keep in mind, at all times, that your body will be sending you signals in response to your movements. You must take note of these signals, be patient and apply just the right amount of pressure in order to avoid an unpleasant experience.

With this in mind, let's go through some of the advanced techniques reflexologists use during regular sessions, for specific conditions. Unlike the simpler movements described previously, these techniques usually involve a routine that can access several reflex areas.

Treating acne

Targeted reflex points: the pituitary, ovary/testicle, adrenal and pancreas.

Acne is most common between the ages of 12 and 24, and is usually associated with an imbalance of hormones, especially during puberty.

To help your body remedy this imbalance, begin the routine by placing your thumb on the pituitary reflex point (at the centre of your big toe, no. 6 on the diagram), pushing in and making circles for 15 seconds. Then, move on to the ovary/testicle reflex point on the lateral side of the foot (no. 60, between the back of the heel and the ankle bone), where you should push gently and use your thumb to make circles for 10 seconds. To stimulate the adrenal reflexes (no. 23, about three steps down from the ball of the foot), place both of your thumbs together on the corresponding point and gently push while making small circles. You should work the adrenals for approximately 15 seconds, before moving to the pancreas reflex point. The latter can be found only on the plantar aspect of the right foot (no. 24, below the third toe). To work this point, place your thumb at the appropriate location and bend it in order to form a hook. Then, use the hook to gauge into it and apply medium pressure as you move your thumb to work the pancreas reflex. This advanced movement is called hooking, and should be applied to the pancreas reflex point for up to 12 seconds.

Ameliorating asthma

Targeted reflex points: the lungs, diaphragm, adrenals, thoracic vertebrae and solar plexus.

Characterized by recurrent episodes of breathlessness, asthma is a lung disease drastically worsened by stress, anxiety and airborne pollutants. During an attack, asthma patients experience coughing, a feeling of tightness in the chest and difficulty in breathing brought about by the constriction and inflammation of the muscle walls within the lungs.

To ameliorate this condition and to decrease the frequency of asthma attacks, begin your routine by working on the lung reflex area (no. 13, on the plantar aspect of the foot). As you flex the foot back to create skin tension with one hand, use your other thumb to work/walk upwards between each of the metatarsals. Repeat this process up to five times. Next, move on to the diaphragm reflex area (no. 17), while continuing to flex the foot. Use small steps to work/walk under the metatarsal heads, across from the lateral to the medial aspect of the foot, and repeat this movement six times. The adrenals should be worked for 15 seconds, as previously described. Then, find the thoracic spine/vertebrae on the lateral aspect of the foot (no. 16) and use 12 steps to work it from the joint of the big toe downwards.

Because each step stimulates a specific vertebra, you should apply light to medium pressure and be very slow as you repeat the movement five times. Finally, move to the solar plexus reflex point (no. 18) and place one thumb at the corresponding location on each foot. As you work this point using small circles, coordinate your movements with your breathing or the breathing of your patient. Breathe in for five seconds, hold your breath for another five and breathe out, as you reduce the pressure on the solar plexus reflex point. Repeat this process six times.

Fighting off constipation

Targeted reflex points: the ascending, sigmoid and descending colon, thyroid and lumbar vertebrae.

Constipation occurs as a result of the slow movement of waste material through the large bowel, possibly caused by an insufficient intake of fibre or fluid, advanced age, some medication or insufficient exercise. Nowadays, constipation is an incredibly common ailment and can result in bad breath, flatulence, headaches, insomnia and even depression.

To ensure a daily, healthy movement of the bowels, begin your reflexology routine with the ascending colon reflex area (no. 33, only on the plantar aspect of the right foot). Stimulate the peristaltic musculature of the colon by walking up this zone from the redness of the heel to halfway up the foot, up to six times. Then, move on to the sigmoid colon reflex area (no. 38, only on the plantar aspect of the left foot) and walk across it six times, just above the redness of the heel. The descending colon reflex area (no. 37) is also unique to the left foot, and should be worked similarly to the ascending colon reflex area. Next, find the thyroid reflex area (no. 11 and 45 on the plantar and, respectively, the dorsal aspects of the foot) and, as you pull back the toes, use your thumb to walk slowly from underneath the ball of the foot all the way up to the neckline, up to seven times. Finally, move to the lumbar vertebrae reflex area, on the lateral aspect of the foot (no. 39). To work it, start walking your thumb from the navicular bone, which corresponds to lumbar one, and take five steps towards the dip in front of the ankle bone, which corresponds to lumbar five. As you reach lumbar five, make small circles for six seconds, and then repeat the movement six times.

Alleviating heartburn

Targeted reflex points: the diaphragm, oesophagus, pancreas, stomach and thoracic vertebrae.

Perceived as a burning pain that moves from the centre of the chest up to the throat, heartburn usually occurs when the muscular sphincter found between the stomach and the oesophagus relaxes and allows the food or digestive juices from the stomach to travel back into the oesophagus. Overeating, eating too quickly, alcohol and rich, fatty or spicy foods are all common causes for heartburn.

To treat this terribly uncomfortable condition, begin your routine at the diaphragm reflex area (no. 17) and repeat the previously described, corresponding movement up to eight times. Next, work the oesophagus reflex area (no. 15, only on the plantar aspect of the left foot) by walking upwards between the metatarsals up to six times. Then, find the pancreas reflex point (no. 24) and work it by making small circles for 10 seconds to help neutralize the unwanted effects of stomach acid. You'll also want to pay attention to the stomach reflex area, just under the ball of the foot (no. 21). Start working this area by walking laterally from the below the thyroid reflex area towards the solar plexus reflex point. As you reach the later, stimulate it with small circles for four seconds, and then repeat the entire process up to eight times. Lastly, stimulate the lateral thoracic vertebrae reflex area (no. 16) up to three times, as previously described.

Preventing osteoporosis

Targeted reflex points: the thyroid, pituitary, parathyroid, hip and spine.

Osteoporosis manifests itself as a weakening of the bones that makes breaking bones more likely, especially with advanced age. The bone mineral density of patients affected by osteoporosis can be reduced by as much as 35%, resulting in porous bones and possible fractures. Elders aged over 60 years are increasingly likely to develop osteoporosis, but an appropriate reflexology routine can help delay and sometimes even prevent this condition.

Begin the routine by working the thyroid reflex area (no. 11 on the plantar aspect and no. 45 on the dorsal aspect of the foot) as described previously for up to one minute. Stimulating this reflex area is essential in fighting off osteoporosis, because it can help control the levels of calcium in the blood. Then, move on to the pituitary reflex point and gently work it for 15 seconds. Next, find the parathyroid reflex point (no. 11, common with the thyroid reflex area) and use your thumb and index fingers to pinch the skin between the big toe and the second toe. As you hold the pressure, gently make circles for 15 seconds in order to help regulate muscle and nerve function, as well as blood calcium levels. To work the hip reflex point (no. 59 on the lateral aspect of the foot), place your thumb on the corresponding area and push in as you make very big circles for 15 seconds. End the routine by working on the entire spine reflex areas on the medial aspect of the foot (no. 8, 16, 39 and 40). Remember that each step corresponds to a specific vertebra, so take your time as you walk from the big toe to the ankle bone. You'll be taking 12 steps alongside the joints of the big toe, 12 steps alongside the foot to the navicular bone and 5 steps towards the dip in front of the ankle bone. Repeat the entire movement three times.

Managing Parkinson's disease

Targeted reflex points: the head, brain, liver, upper lymphatics, adrenals and spine.

Parkinson's is a degenerative disease that affects the nervous system and usually restricts the transmission of messages between one nerve cell and another. Although the underlying cause is still unknown, an estimated 10 million people live with this disabling condition worldwide. A cure does not exist for Parkinson's disease, but regular reflexology sessions can improve the wellbeing of the sufferer and might even prevent further degeneration of the nervous system. However, this disorder is commonly associated with movement disabilities, which means that reflexology sessions can only be completed with the help of a friend, family member or professional.

Begin the session by working on the head reflex area, which is located on the plantar aspect of the big toe. For one minute, support the big toe with one hand and use your other thumb to walk upwards from the neckline to the top. Then, focus on the brain reflex areas (no. 1) by slowly walking along the top of the toes for up to twelve times. As you move on to the liver reflex area (no. 19, only on the plantar aspect of the right foot), place your thumb laterally, just underneath the ball of the foot and work slowly towards the middle of the foot on a horizontal line. Then, move your thumb lower and repeat. Complete the entire movement up to five times before continuing to the upper lymphatics reflex areas (no. 48 and 49 on the dorsal aspect of the foot). To work on the latter, place your index finger on the dorsal aspect of the foot and your thumb on the plantar aspect, between the metatarsals. Use both fingers to walk down from the base of the toes towards the ankle, as far as you can reach. As you slide back, make circles lightly. This movement should be repeated up to four times, followed by 15 seconds of working the adrenal reflex point. Finally, complete the routine by working on the entire spine up to four times, as previously described.

Chapter 10

Complementary healing to reflexology

As you will certainly find out if you decide to undergo regular reflexology sessions and, indeed, the most important aspect to take away from this brief outline is the fact that reflexology promotes a holistic approach to health. While different routines performed by an experienced practitioner will undoubtedly improve your condition and your state of mind, it is important to remember that reflexology cannot offer a cure to any specific disease. What it does offer is something much healthier than pharmaceuticals, by enhancing your body's natural healing abilities and helping it overcome any kind of harmful unbalance. In other words, reflexology can support your body in doing what it was naturally designed to do.

But routines alone do not achieve the full potential of reflexology. To complement them, practitioners usually recommend lifestyle changes that take a holistic approach to the patient's healing process. These changes are deemed healthy by both conventional and holistic doctors, which means that you have only to gain in trying them out. On a minimal level, they concern a healthy exercise program, a diverse, nutritive diet and positive ways of coping with daily stress and anxiety. Let's take a closer look at a few illustrative examples.

Exercise

Time and time again, the benefits of exercise have been demonstrated through competent studies or in the day-to-day lives of ordinary people. As holistic practitioners, reflexologists have supported exercise as part of the body's healing process throughout the years, and at this point, the positive health implications of regular physical activity have become very difficult to ignore.

Some benefits, such as preventing excess weight gain or combating a wide range of health problems, are more obvious than others. For instance, exercising regularly for at least 30 minutes three times a week can reduce your risk of cardiovascular disease by as much as 40%. Many other diseases and concerns, like stroke, type 2 diabetes, depression and even certain kinds of cancer become more manageable through exercise. Not yet convinced? Think of the benefits of exercise for your mood, your confidence and your self-esteem. There's nothing like a good workout or a pleasant walk to lift the spirits and boost your energy levels. As your lungs and heart develop thanks to your physical activity, you'll have more stamina throughout the day and you'll sleep better at night.

What is even more surprising is the fact that we are now discovering the less-known benefits of exercise on our minds. As it turns out, although for a long time we believed physical activity was solely advantageous for our bodies, we know today that it can help prevent cognitive decline, improve overall brain performance, sharpen memory and even boost creativity. Reflexologists are aware of this, and will recommend an exercise routine that is suitable for you, as well as easy to include in your daily schedule. And it doesn't have to be boring! Some people enjoy working out in a gym or building muscle mass, but others do not. If you're one of the latter, don't think that you're out of options. If you love spending time outdoors, walking, trailing, hiking, climbing and riding the bike are all great physical activities for you. If you have an outgoing personality, then you could consider taking up a team sport or even a competitive sport such as tennis or badminton. You might not want to spend as much time exercising, but you could choose to create a short, 30 minutes aerobics routine for many of the same benefits. Trying out some beginner's yoga or Pilates routines might also be a good idea. All in all, the possibilities are numerous and, with the appropriate guidance, you are categorically bound to find something that is both fun and beneficial for your body.

Diet

How often have we heard the phrase "you are what you eat"? It's not surprising, then, that scientific evidence is mounting in favour of the presumption that our diets significantly affect our health and wellbeing. Reflexologists recognize that the common Western diet can take a toll on health, effectively laying the foundation for several diseases. A poor diet, riddled with high amounts of processed or refined foods, as well as additives that are toxic for the human body, will inevitably cumulate to a great deal of stress of the body's processes, eventually weakening organs and creating a blood composition that is excessively acid or otherwise imbalanced.

To help your body heal from an ailment, taking small steps in improving your diet can go a tremendous way.

But first, let's get more acquainted to some of the foods we are very familiar with, and their impact on our health. Sugar, for instance, can be completely devoid of vitamins and nutrients in its most concentrated forms. It causes a surge in blood sugar levels and disrupts the hormonal balance of the body, while reducing your ability to fight off infection by as much as 50%. Another familiar example is coffee, which has received much attention lately in regard to its alleged health benefits. While coffee might be rich in antioxidants, this does not in any way improve the fact that it has been associated with high cholesterol levels, headaches, insomnia, heart palpitations and anxiety. Similarly, processed meat or cheese can be found in almost anyone's fridge, but the truth is that they have been repeatedly associated with many serious diseases, including certain types of cancer, type 2 diabetes and heart disease.

At first, it might sound rather scary to give up all of these foods, mainly because they have likely been part of your life for as long as you can remember. With small steps, however, no change is too intimidating. For instance, you could replace the sugary, processed cereal you have in the morning with a healthy bowl of cooked oatmeal. Certain types of oatmeal can be very yummy and only take 10 minutes to cook, so you wouldn't even notice the difference. Your body, on the other hand, definitely would. Instead of causing a surge, oatmeal would stabilize your blood sugar and make you feel full throughout a longer period of time. As another example, what about switching from white bread to whole-grain, its much healthier alternative? It's small steps like these that can make a world of a difference for your body. Moreover, as your body reaches balance, poor quality foods that you thought you couldn't live without will no longer appeal to you.

To begin with, it is essential to acknowledge that by making small adjustments to your diet, you can truly help your body and, as a result, change the way you feel for the better. A competent reflexologist will be able to guide you through this process as you attend regular sessions. Otherwise, you can always speak to a nutritionist about taking your very first steps towards a healthier eating plan.

Stress and Anxiety

Stress is the body's response to a threat or a dangerous situation, while the changes it causes in our bodies used to make sense thousands of years ago when we were constantly faced with fight or flight situations. It is odd that in an age where security and life expectancy have increased tremendously, we are permanently plagued by stress. And yet, this is the case now more than ever. During stress, your body is designed to increase your strength and speed, but if you are not actually physically active, these effects can be devastating for your health.

For instance, in order to generate energy, the body calls on fat reserves and releases fatty deposits in the blood. Most often than not, we do not actually use these resources because we are not faced with a situation where we must be physically active. This means that the fatty deposits stay in the blood and ultimately contribute to arteriosclerosis and an increased risk of heart disease. A similar process takes place with glucose, which is released by the liver in dangerous amounts in situations of stress, remains in the bloodstream and eventually leads to diabetes. Furthermore, the steroid hormone cortisone is released by the adrenal glands in large quantities, which, in the long run, can be toxic for the brain and cause depression and memory loss. These are just some of the side effects of stress, and when you consider our modern, hectic lifestyles, it's easy to see that the consequences on our bodies can be overwhelming.

Regular reflexology sessions can help you relieve stress, but it's also a good idea to adopt a few practical help mechanisms that can calm you down between sessions, in times of stress or anxiety. A common help practice recommended by reflexologists is deep-breathing, which you can discreetly try throughout the day in order to relax your body. You can also learn to accompany your breathing techniques with positive affirmations that will help you escape a negative mindset. Come up with a few positive statements that represent what you would like to happen in your life or within your body, and repeat these statements in the morning or at any time when you feel distressed. As your reflexologist will explain, it is essential to find positive ways of dealing with stress by taking an active approach and not allowing it to take over your life.

Slowly, but surely, you'll notice that small changes in all of these aspects of your life will have a beneficial effect on your state of mind and on your health. Feel free to practice different reflexology techniques described here on yourself or a friend, but always bear in mind that reflexology involves a holistic approach to health and calls for a healthier lifestyle throughout. Unlike many conventional doctors, a reflexology practitioner will interact with you on a personal level and will seek to identify and help improve your particular condition. It's only natural, then, that they will try to help you better the quality of your life in general by guiding you through exercise, a healthy diet and positive ways to cope with the frenetic contemporary lifestyle. Hopefully, with their professional help, as well as with the information contained in this brief description of reflexology, you'll come even closer to achieving both your physical and emotional life goals.

36077999R00066

Printed in Great Britain
by Amazon